Hiraeth

AF624520

A.G. Clementine

BookLeaf Publishing

Presentation by *BookLeaf Publishing*

Web: www.bookleafpub.com

E-mail: info@bookleafpub.com

ISBN: 9789357445375

First edition 2022

DEDICATION

To my future self, I hope you are happy and at peace.

PREFACE

A collection of poems written during the ups and downs of my life. I hope next year I can look back upon them and smile.

Take me home

Take me home
To the gardens full of life
To the geraniums and hyacinths
To the daffodils dancing in the spring breeze

Take me home
Where laughter and joy roar out of the windows
Where love is plenty, and hatred is less
To where it is a beacon of hope and a safe haven
in the storm

Oh, take me home.

Dream

When life has passed in a blink of an eye
When you have drank sorrows in gallons and happiness in trifles
When you detest the sound of home, as it brings you nothing but pain
When life and death don't seem any different, dream

Dream so that the pain goes away
Dream of a better life

One with happiness, love, and peace
Where the good time outweigh the bad
Dream of a kind, supportive and caring family
Where you are unaccustomed to sadness and grief

Dream and believe
And, if you dream hard enough
I promise you will be living that dream soon
Alive and real
Alive and thriving
Alive with love and peace.

Strong, powerful, and undefeated

Under the roaring sky
Where the thunder bellows
And lightning flashes
I find peace.

Where the wind howls
The rain pours, the cold penetrating in
Bringing a chill to the bone
I feel alive.

When the heavens pour down in gallons
And the thunder is deafening
When the electrifying lightning crackles
I don't run and hide

I absorb the energy, the might, and the fear
As the cold raindrops pierce my skin
I feel like I've been born again

Like the pain has been washed away
Like the sky is with me, calling me
Giving me its strength.

The wind, thunder, lightning, and rain
They are me, And I am them
Strong, powerful, and undefeated.

The Past

The past, I can't seem to remember
It seems to have passed in a blink of an eye
The moments captured in pictures seem like
fragments of my imagination

I don't seem to recall them, they seem like they
never happened.
The past seems like another life I had,
Something which is not familiar

Something which doesn't any connection with
me
What was the truth and what were the lies?
No that can't have happened, how am I still
living then?

I'm meant to be full of life, joyful and kind
Something I always was
Or was I not?

Surely, it was only yesterday I was playing in
the park
Singing in the choir and riding my bicycle
Oh but that was years ago

So innocent and hidden from the evils of the
world and black hearted humans and the
unfortunate timing of fate
Oh just take me back.

The Storm

All of this is a bad dream
A dream I'll awaken from surely
If not, then why does God insist me on living
Then why haven't I withered away from the
amount of grief and pain life has given me?

It's a storm that I'm stuck in for years
But I'll dance in the rain still
I will stay strong and withstand whatever life
throws at me

What if this is God?
What if I'm cursed to have a bad life?
What if I do deserve it?
What if God is punishing me?

No, God loves me and wants me to get through
this raging tempest.
Go on, bring the worst of it all
I will sing
I will dance
I will run
And I'll get through it all

I'll absorb the good and bad
Transforming me into an unbreakable
Joyful, caring
Kind and trustworthy person

And when the first robin chirps after this storm
I'll be alive
Alive and smiling
Alive and well.

Caged

While the world was caged
She grew blossoms in her heart

They blossomed from grief
Anger
Loneliness
And countless times of giving up

But just see her now in the spring
Tall and beautiful.

Life's Little Pleasures

What a beautiful life it would be
To hear the falling off the delicate Sakura
Into the last stages of their life
Beautiful and timeless.

Familiarity

On a cold rainy day
The young lady came again
With pockets full of a peanuts
I welcomed her again
Thanking her to remember us
I hope to see her again.

Over The Horizon

Somewhere over the horizon
In a place of ember and ashes
Where water is aflame
You'll find me waiting

In a place where
Darkness and lies
Deceit and betrayal
Sorrow and despair

Are always there
I'll be waiting patiently
For the end of it all.

Flowers and Rain

She's beautiful like flowers
But she's also rain

She's the beauty of the day
But also nights full of pain

And everyday she wakes up with a smile
In hopes of a brighter day.

Cappuccino

Those sparkling ice blue eyes
Carried the beauty of the oceans and skies
They carried the struggle of life
Knew stories more than a few

Of love, grief and despair
But those ice blue eyes
They were enough to warm anyone
On a cold winter night

With cold rain and warm, cozy Cappuccino, who needs anything more?

Mid-Summer Breeze

I used to believe
That life would be happiness and bliss
That I'll be counting away the stars on a hilltop
And sleeping under the sky each night

With the windows down and the speakers on
We'll be climbing up the mountainous terrain
On a summer trip through the clouds
While swaying with the mid-summer breeze

Oh, what a lie it has all been
But what a journey it's been

One full of happiness and sorrow
Entwined together they have filled my life with bittersweet moments
Oh what a life it's been.

What People Say

Life will get better they say
But it seems that I've spent my whole life
listening to this phrase

Life is it worth it, they say
But all the people that make life living seem to
go away

Life is full of love, they say
But all that life gave me was thorns and pains

Life is … something I want to run away from
and never feel again.

Fairytale Princess

Oh to be running barefoot in the woods
Free as a bird
With the earth beneath my feet
And the wind across my face

Oh what a life would it be

In The Spring

I hope to see you in the spring
Rejuvenated and Grown
Grown and Alive, that is.

Story Of My Life

Isn't it strange that in a blink of an eye
You can be around the world
Starting a new life
Like the past had forgotten itself

Next Spring

It's been quite sometime
Since i've spoken my mind
Well, what can I say
It's been a whale of a ride

Now home is different..
A place of joy? Maybe….
A place of pain, oh for sure
But my home is under construction

Just wait and see it next spring
It'll be overflowing with flowers

With joy pouring out of the windows
With no place for pain to dwell
I'll be happy you'll see
I'll be alive that is, if only.

If Only

If only, pain and sorrow won't know our address
If only, we're lucky and happiness comes to stay

If only, life gets better in a way that makes us
forget our pain
If only, the past is erased.

If only, love and joy finds their way into our
home again.
If only, the darkness in my mind doesn't put out
that tiny spark of light.

And if only it doesn't devour me till my last
speck of strength
If only, life was a piece of cake I'd say.

October

The air is cold and crisp
With a different aura to it all
The wind is strong and chilly
With the first shower pouring in

The sun is peeking behind the clouds
With a feeling of comfort in its warmth
The ground is littered with leaves,
Turning golden from green

With a symphony to our ears when we crisp
those wilting leaves
A walk in the park is all we need
The array of colors which is hard to believe
It's a feast for the eyes indeed

With the first chills of winter settling in
I take a breath of relief
Snuggling onto the sofa
With my hot chocolate and a piece of carrot cake

I mark the beginning of winter
Oh, what a year indeed.

My Past Self

Little girl
You're still naïve and young
Still playing in a fairytale with no fear from the world
You have no idea what's going to happen

But trust me, it's for the better
Just pretend it's one gulp of sour medicine

You and me
We are so alike
And different in so many ways
We're going to change, for the better, for the future, for us

Young girl
We're going to get through it in the end
I promise you
Don't lose hope and never stop believing
I promise it's going to be okay

No matter how many times you tumble, cry and fall
It's going to be okay
Everything will turn out better in the end

I promise you

Young woman
We'll be smiling in the end
After the storm
Standing and laughing
Playing and living

We'll get there in the end
I promise you

www.ingramcontent.com/pod-product-compliance
Lightning Source LLC
Chambersburg PA
CBHW051756130826
49812CB00033B/1182
* 9 7 8 9 3 5 7 4 4 5 3 7 5 *